THE BEST JOB EVER

Pop Star

Ian F. Mahaney

PowerKiDS press.

New York

Published in 2015 by The Rosen Publishing Group, Inc.
29 East 21st Street, New York, NY 10010

First Edition

Editor: Caitie McAneney
Book Design: Katelyn Heinle

Photo Credits: Cover, pp. 3–24 (background design) Toria/Shutterstock.com; cover (boy) Adam Taylor/Photodisc/Getty Images; p. 5 spirit of america/ Shutterstock.com; pp. 6, 19 Everett Collection/Shutterstock.com; p. 7 http://commons.wikimedia.org/wiki/File:Andy_Grammer_2014.jpg; p. 8 s_bukley/Shutterstock.com; p. 9 Donald Kravitz/Getty Images Entertainment/ Getty Images; p. 11 bikeriderlondon/Shutterstock.com; p. 13 Jeff Kravitz/AMA2010/ FilmMagic, Inc/Getty Images; p. 15 John Shearer/WireImage/Getty Images; p. 16 George De Sota/Redferns/Getty Images; p. 17 (top) photosthatrock/ Shutterstock.com; p. 17 (bottom) Theo Wargo/WireImage/Getty Images; p. 18 Featureflash/Shutterstock.com; p. 20 Kevin Mazur/Wire Image/ Getty Images; p. 21 Rick Diamond/Getty Images Entertainment/Getty Images; p. 22 Mark Davis/Getty Images Entertainment/Getty Images.

Library of Congress Cataloging-in-Publication Data

Mahaney, Ian F.
Pop star / by Ian F. Mahaney.
p. cm. — (The best job ever)
Includes index.
ISBN 978-1-4994-0128-8 (pbk.)
ISBN 978-1-4994-0084-7 (6-pack)
ISBN 978-1-4994-0107-3 (library binding)
1. Popular music — Vocational guidance — Juvenile literature. I. Mahaney, Ian F. II. Title.
ML3795.M34 2015
781.64023—d23

Manufactured in the United States of America

CPSIA Compliance Information: Batch #CW15PK: For Further Information contact Rosen Publishing, New York, New York at 1-800-237-9932

Contents

A GLAMOROUS LIFE

Do you love to sing and dance? Would you like to be featured on the cover of a magazine? Can you imagine having thousands of people shouting your name at a **concert**? That's the **glamorous** life of a pop star!

Pop stars are people who **perform** popular music, or pop. Some perform alone, while others perform as part of a band.

Pop stars first rose to fame when radio and television became popular. Fans loved Elvis Presley in the 1950s and went crazy for the Beatles in the 1960s. Who are some of today's famous pop stars?

Pop stars like Katy Perry sing and dance in sold-out shows around the world.

AN AMAZING CAREER

Being a pop star can be a fun **career**, especially if you love to sing and dance for an **audience**. Some pop stars even get to act on television or in movies! They have the opportunity to travel around the world and meet many people. They can raise awareness for important causes, and many people listen to their opinions. Best of all, they're paid a lot of money to create new and exciting music.

It's a lot of hard work to get this amazing job. An **aspiring** pop star has to learn how to sing, dance, and sometimes play musical instruments.

POP STAR BIO: BEYONCÉ

Beyoncé began her career as a member of the group Destiny's Child in the 1990s. In 2003, she released her first **solo** album. She's well-known for her songs "Single Ladies" and "Irreplaceable." She also acts in movies, including *Dreamgirls*.

It can take a lot of luck to "break into the business" of pop music. Andy Grammer played his music on the street as a **busker** until he became famous.

SCHOOL, LESSONS, AND PRACTICE

It takes a lot of practice to make it far in the music business. Many pop stars start their career early by learning music and dance skills. You can take singing lessons with a voice coach from a young age. You can also join a dance **studio** to learn how to follow **routines**. Lady Gaga started playing piano when she was only four years old!

Lady Gaga went to musical theater school at New York University (NYU) when she was only 17 years old. She learned about songwriting, other singers in history, and art.

Madonna

Some pop stars study singing and dancing in high school and college. That's where they can learn more advanced skills. Madonna, a pop star who rose to fame in the 1980s, studied dance in high school and college.

RISING TO FAME

When you see pop stars on stage, you might think they were born famous. But each started as a beginner who put in a lot of time and work. Justin Bieber taught himself to sing and play drums, piano, and guitar before he became famous.

Pop stars rise to fame by gaining fans. Some aspiring pop stars make videos of themselves playing music to gain fans online. Others gain fans as buskers.

An aspiring pop star's goal is to get a music manager. Managers help the musician get a **record deal**. After this, the aspiring star's music could be on its way to the radio!

Some aspiring pop stars will use their own money to record their music in a studio. They'll do anything to have their music heard!

FINDING A MENTOR

A young musician can have all the skill it takes to be a pop star. They may think they know everything about the business, and they may even have a manager. But sometimes the musician needs to find a mentor to help guide them into fame.

A mentor is a skilled **professional** who helps someone through new situations, especially a new career. A mentor can help an aspiring pop star learn new skills and practice what they know. They can help the person meet important people in the music business. Mentors can also make their own fans get excited about the new star.

Justin Bieber's mentor was Usher, a pop star who has spent many years in the music business. Bieber found his mentor when he was just 13 years old.

SINGING

Pop stars make singing in concert look easy, but it takes a lot of practice. Most pop stars have voice coaches who help them work on their **vocal range**. They often want to create a sound that's fresh and new, to set them apart from other pop stars.

Some pop stars write the words, or lyrics, to their own songs. These musicians are called singer-songwriters. Other pop stars sing covers, or songs another singer has already made famous. Still other pop stars sing songs written by professional songwriters. A professional songwriter writes songs with the pop star's style of music in mind.

Adele is a famous singer-songwriter. She released the song "Chasing Pavements" in 2008 and soon became well-known for her great lyrics and original voice.

BUST A MOVE!

Dancing is often a huge part of a pop star's performance. Some pop stars don't dance in their acts, but knowing how to dance often helps an aspiring pop star's career.

Most people can learn to dance. Dance teachers help people learn the skills they need to dance well. Choreographers plan routines for pop stars and teach them the dance for a concert. Bruno Mars is a pop star who's known for his dance routines in concert. He has backup dancers, too. Mars's choreographer makes sure he and his backup dancers are always in step with each other.

POP STAR BIO: MICHAEL JACKSON

Michael Jackson's nickname was the King of Pop. He started his music career with his brothers as part of the Jackson Five in the 1960s. He then made his own solo act in the 1980s and became famous for his songs and dance moves.

Dancing was very important to pop bands in the 1990s. The Backstreet Boys used dance routines as a main part of their concerts.

OUT ON TOUR

Pop stars earn most of their money on tour. A tour is a chain of concerts in different cities. Pop stars often play in big buildings where shows and sporting events are held, called arenas. The arena sells tickets for the concerts. The arena then pays the pop star a portion of the money they make.

The length of a tour and the size of the arenas depends on the popularity of the star. In 2014, Lady Gaga performed at huge arenas in more than 50 cities worldwide. She played in North America, Europe, Asia, and Australia.

POP STAR BIO: JUSTIN TIMBERLAKE

Justin Timberlake broke into pop music when he joined a famous boy band called 'N Sync in the 1990s. He started his solo act in 2002, and he became well-known for his pop songs, such as "Mirrors" and "Suit & Tie." He's also a movie star.

Pop stars on tour travel around the world,
playing shows for days in a row. Justin Timberlake
played over 100 shows in 2014!

JOBS IN POP MUSIC

Many jobs are related to a pop star's career. A pop star will have a manager who guides them through the business side of music. A pop star likely has an agent. An agent helps a pop star put together tours and makes sure they're getting enough money.

Beyoncé

Bruno Mars

Other musicians, singers, and dancers support the star. Think of the backup dancers who perform with Bruno Mars or Justin Timberlake. In a studio, producers help a pop star record music and make an album. Even if an aspiring pop star can't take center stage, he or she can still work with a pop star.

Do you love to dance? A job as a choreographer or backup dancer for the stars could be a great job!

Being a pop star can be a perfect career for someone who loves music. Pop stars can be creative, and they're known for their original talent and style.

Not everyone can be a pop star, but many people can make it as musicians. To do this, you have to study music, especially music history and how to perform. You should take voice lessons or learn an instrument, such as guitar or piano. To increase your chances of being a pop star, you can also study dance, especially hip hop dance. Who knows? You could be a pop star some day!

Pharrell Williams

Glossary

aspiring: Strongly wanting to achieve a goal.

audience: A group of people gathered to see or hear something.

busker: Someone who performs in a public place, such as a sidewalk.

career: A job.

concert: An event where live music is played.

glamorous: Full of excitement, wealth, or fame.

perform: To play music or present something for people to enjoy.

professional: Someone who is paid for what they do.

record deal: A lawful agreement between a recording business and a musician.

routine: A worked-out part of an activity.

solo: Something that is done on one's own.

studio: A place to work on dancing, singing, or art.

vocal range: The measure of notes a singer's voice can hit.

Index

Websites

Due to the changing nature of Internet links, PowerKids Press has developed an online list of websites related to the subject of this book. This site is updated regularly. Please use this link to access the list: www.powerkidslinks.com/bje/pops